40 Of The Most Requested Classical Pieces Of All Time

Includes Cello Concerto, Clarinet Concerto, The Pearl Fishers (Duet), Pie Jesu, Flower Duet, plus many more!

This book © Copyright 2006 Amsco Publications,

All Rights Reserved. Unauthorized reproduction of any part of this publication
by any means including photocopying is an infringement of copyright.

Order No. AM987943

ISBN-13: 978-1-84609-794-2

40 Of The Most Requested Classical Pieces Of All Time

EXCLUSIVELY DISTRIBUTED BY

HAL•LEONARD®

Air On The G String page 6
(from 'Suite No.3') Bach

Ave Maria page 8
Schubert

The Blue Danube page 12
Strauss

Canon in D page 10
Pachelbel

Carmen page 15
Bizet

Cello Concerto page 18
(First Movement Theme) Elgar

Clair de Lune page 21
(from 'Suite Bergamasque') Debussy

Clarinet Concerto page 24
(Second Movement Theme) Mozart

Dance Of The Sugar Plum Fairy page 53
(from 'The Nutcracker') Tchaikovsky

Eine kleine Nachtmusik page 26
(First Movement Theme) Mozart

Enigma Variations page 30
(Nimrod) Elgar

Flower Duet page 32
(from 'Lakme') Delibes

The Four Seasons page 34
('Autumn' Third movement) Vivaldi

Für Elise page 36
Beethoven

Gymnopédie No.1 page 38
Satie

Hallelujah Chorus page 40
(from 'The Messiah') Handel

Jesu, Joy Of Man's Desiring page 43
Bach

La Donna é Mobile page 48
(from 'Rigoletto') Verdi

Land Of Hope And Glory page 50
(Pomp and Circumstance March No.1) Elgar

Liebesträume page 56
Liszt

Miserere page 58
Allegri

Moonlight Sonata page 62
(First Movement Theme) Beethoven

Morning page 65
(from 'Peer Gynt') Grieg

Ode To Joy page 68
(from Symphony No.9 'Choral' Fourth Movement) Beethoven

Panis Angelicus page 70
Franck

The Pearl Fishers page 73
(Duet: 'Au Fond Du Temple Saint') Bizet

Piano Concerto No.2 page 76
(Second Movement Theme) Chopin

Piano Concerto No.21 'Elvira Madigan' page 82
(Second Movement Theme) Mozart

Pictures At An Exhibition page 84
(Promenade) Mussorgsky

Pie Jesu page 79
(from 'Requiem' Op.48') Fauré

The Planets page 88
(Jupiter) Holst

Swan Lake page 86
(Waltz) Tchaikovsky

Symphony No.5 page 89
(First Movement Theme) Beethoven

Symphony No.5 page 94
(Fourth Movement Theme) Mahler

Symphony No.6 'Pastoral' page 97
(Finale Theme) Beethoven

Symphony No.8 'Unfinished' page 100
(First Movement Theme) Schubert

Violin Concerto No.1 page 101
(Second Movement Theme) Bruch

Waltz Of The Flowers page 108
(from 'The Nutcracker') Tchaikovsky

Water Music page 104
(Air) Handel

William Tell: Overture page 106
Rossini

Air On The G String

(from Suite No.3)

Music by Johann Sebastian Bach

Slow

© Copyright 2006 Dorsey Brothers Music Limited.
All Rights Reserved. International Copyright Secured.

Ave Maria

Music by Franz Schubert

Moderately slow

© Copyright 2006 Dorsey Brothers Music Limited.
All Rights Reserved. International Copyright Secured.

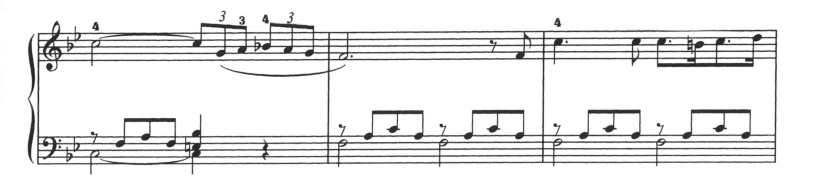

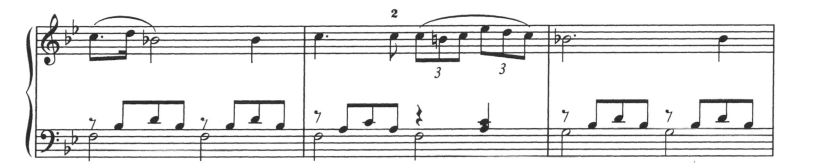

Canon in D

Music by Johann Pachelbel

Moderately

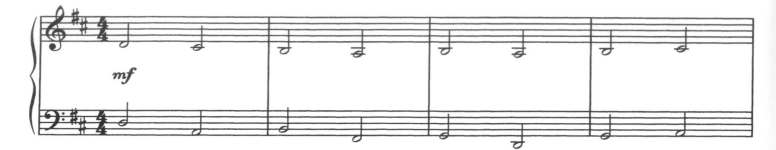

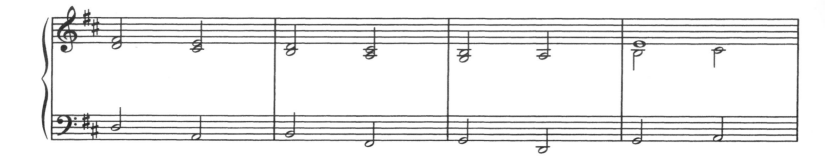

© Copyright 2006 Dorsey Brothers Music Limited.
All Rights Reserved. International Copyright Secured.

11

The Blue Danube

Music by Johann Strauss

Waltz

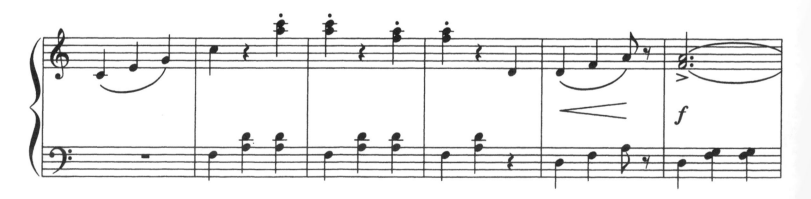

© Copyright 2006 Dorsey Brothers Music Limited.
All Rights Reserved. International Copyright Secured.

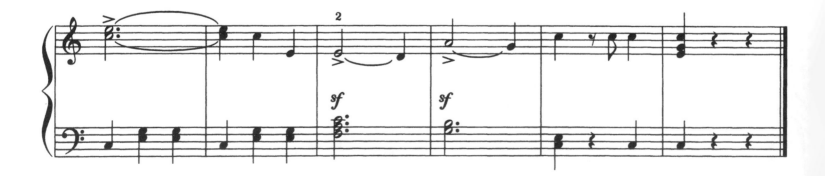

14

Carmen

(Habanera)

Music by Georges Bizet

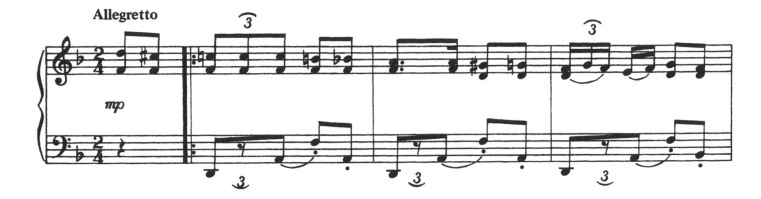

© Copyright 2006 Dorsey Brothers Music Limited.
All Rights Reserved. International Copyright Secured.

Cello Concerto
(First Movement Theme)

Music by Edward Elgar

Adagio

Moderato

© Copyright 2006 Dorsey Brothers Music Limited.
All Rights Reserved. International Copyright Secured.

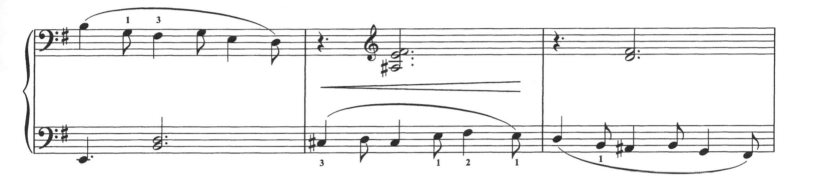

poco allargando

Clair de Lune
(from Suite Bergamasque)

Music by Claude Debussy

Moderately

© Copyright 2006 Dorsey Brothers Music Limited.
All Rights Reserved. International Copyright Secured.

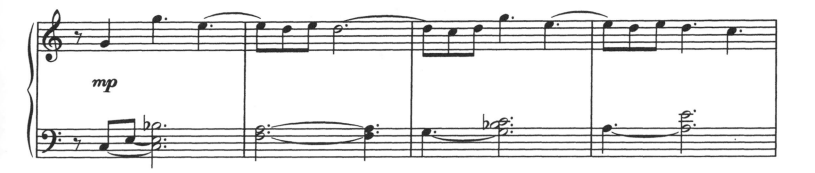

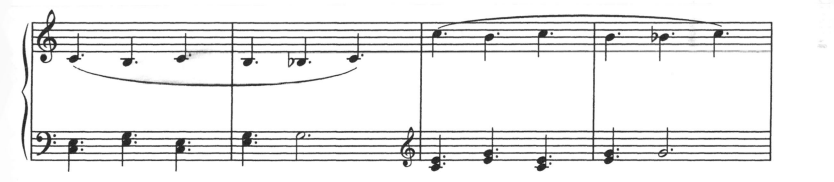

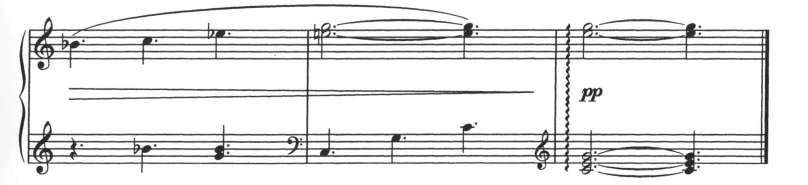

Clarinet Concerto
(Second Movement Theme)

Music by Wolfgang Amadeus Mozart

Slow

© Copyright 2006 Dorsey Brothers Music Limited.
All Rights Reserved. International Copyright Secured.

Eine kleine Nachtmusik

(First Movement Theme)

Music by Wolfgang Amadeus Mozart

Allegro

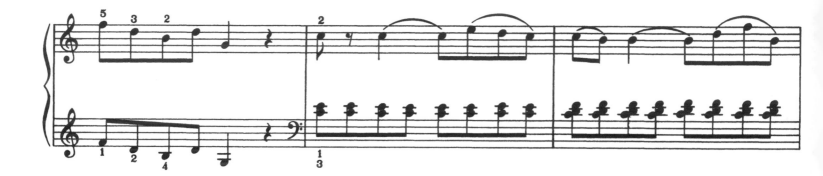

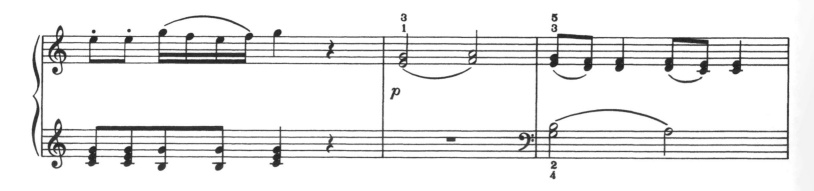

© Copyright 2006 Dorsey Brothers Music Limited.
All Rights Reserved. International Copyright Secured.

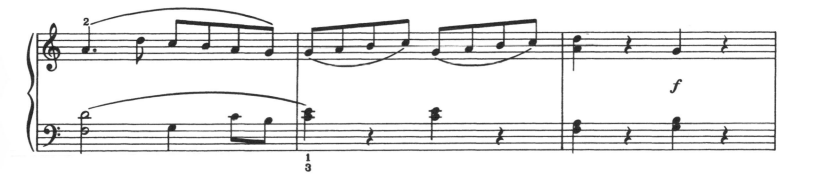

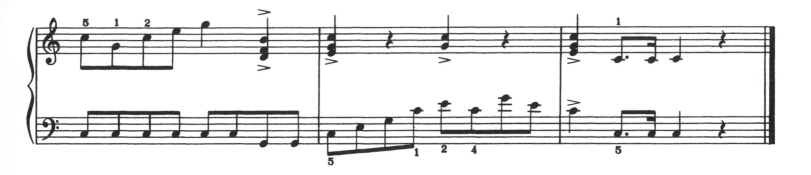

Enigma Variations
(Nimrod)

Music by Edward Elgar

Slow

© Copyright 2006 Dorsey Brothers Music Limited.
All Rights Reserved. International Copyright Secured.

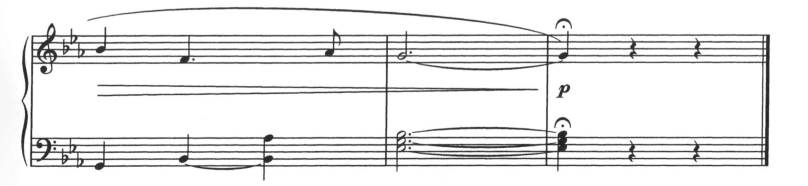

Flower Duet
(from Lakmé)

Music by Leo Delibes

Moderately

© Copyright 2006 Dorsey Brothers Music Limited.
All Rights Reserved. International Copyright Secured.

The Four Seasons
(Third Movement Theme, 'Autumn')

Music by Antonio Vivaldi

Allegro

© Copyright 2006 Dorsey Brothers Music Limited.
All Rights Reserved. International Copyright Secured.

Für Elise

Music by Ludwig Van Beethoven

Moderately

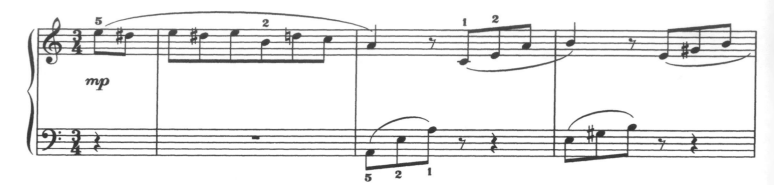

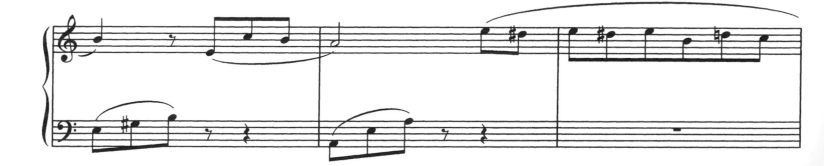

© Copyright 2006 Dorsey Brothers Music Limited.
All Rights Reserved. International Copyright Secured.

Gymnopédie No.1

Music by Erik Satie

Slow

© Copyright 2006 Dorsey Brothers Music Limited.
All Rights Reserved. International Copyright Secured.

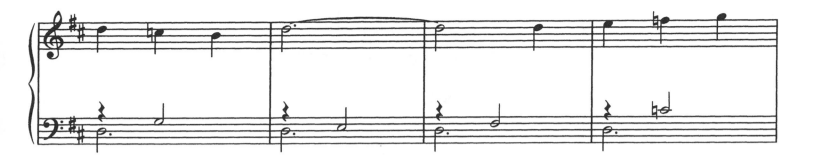

39

Hallelujah Chorus
(from The Messiah)

Music by George Frideric Handel

© Copyright 2006 Dorsey Brothers Music Limited.
All Rights Reserved. International Copyright Secured.

Jesu, Joy Of Man's Desiring

Music by Johann Sebastian Bach

Moderately

© Copyright 2006 Dorsey Brothers Music Limited.
All Rights Reserved. International Copyright Secured.

La Donna é Mobile

(from Rigoletto)

Music by Giuseppe Verdi

Moderately

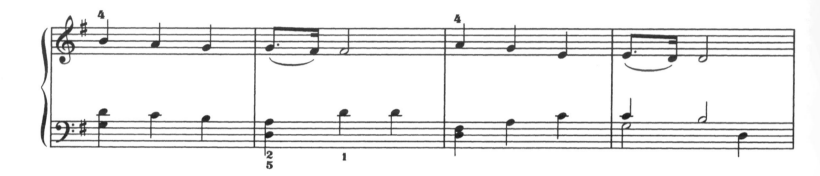

© Copyright 2006 Dorsey Brothers Music Limited.
All Rights Reserved. International Copyright Secured.

49

'Land Of Hope And Glory'
Pomp And Circumstance March No.1

Music by Edward Elgar

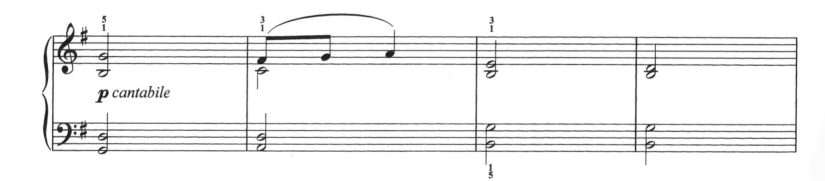

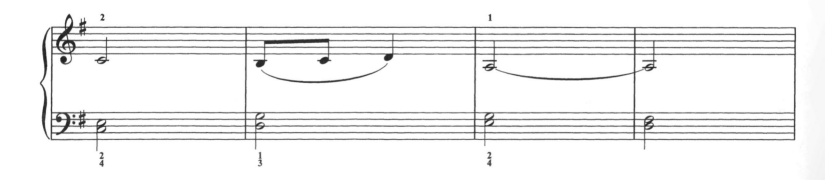

© Copyright 2006 Dorsey Brothers Music Limited.
All Rights Reserved. International Copyright Secured.

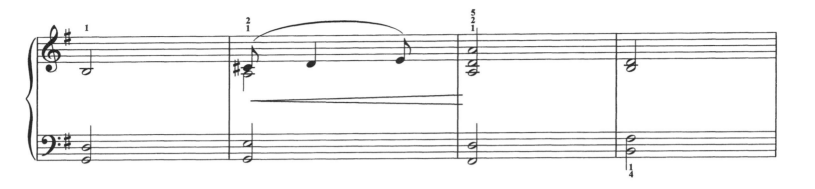

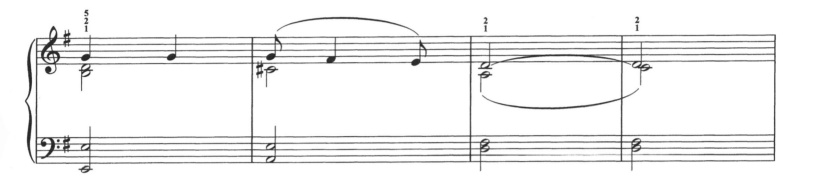

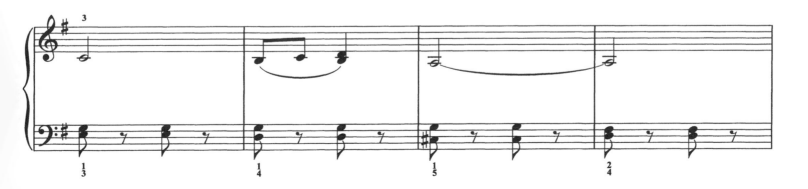

Dance Of The Sugar Plum Fairy
(from The Nutcracker)

Music by Peter Ilyich Tchaikovsky

Andante non troppo

© Copyright 2006 Dorsey Brothers Music Limited.
All Rights Reserved. International Copyright Secured.

Liebesträume

Music by Franz Liszt

© Copyright 2006 Dorsey Brothers Music Limited.
All Rights Reserved. International Copyright Secured.

ritard.   *a tempo*

ritard.

Miserere

Music by Gregorio Allegri

Slowly and solemnly ♩ = 100

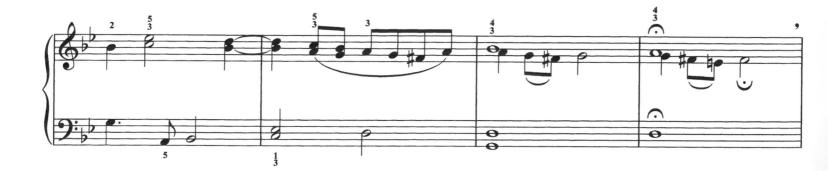

© Copyright 2006 Dorsey Brothers Music Limited.
All Rights Reserved. International Copyright Secured.

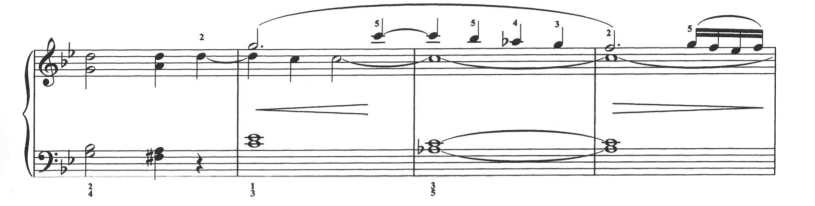

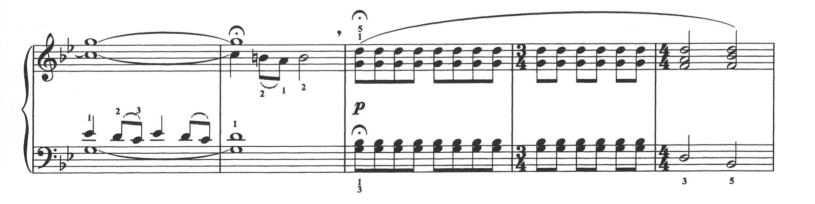

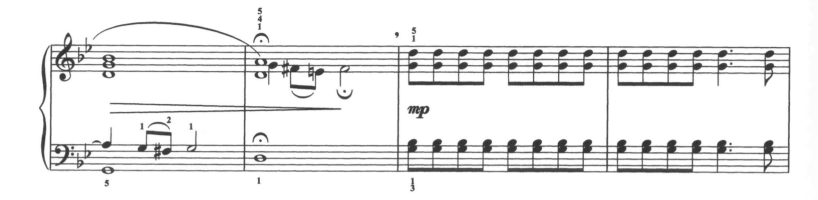

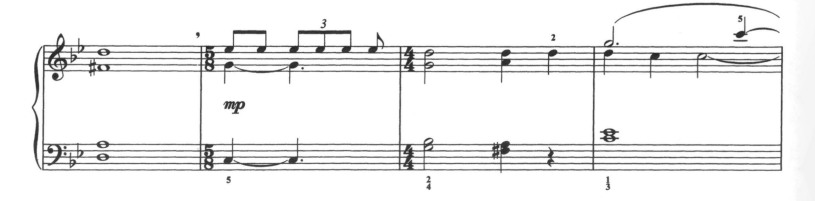

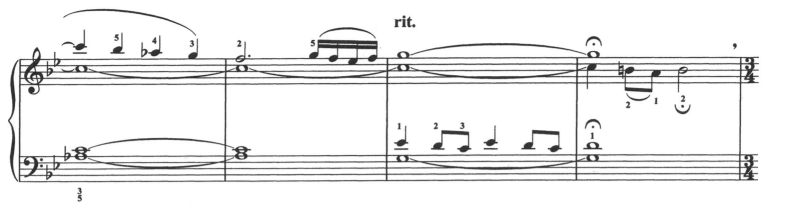

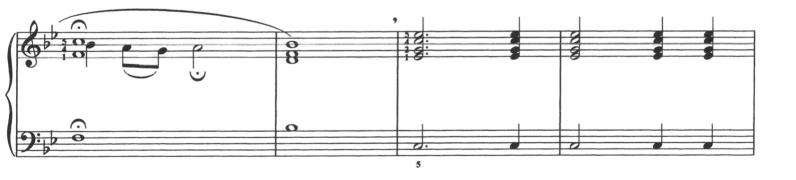

61

'Moonlight' Sonata
(First Movement)

Music by Ludwig Van Beethoven

Slowly

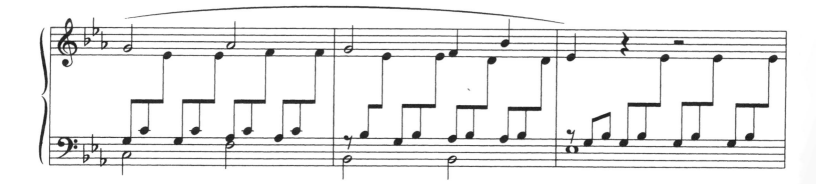

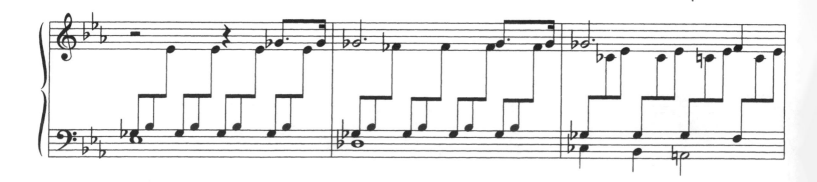

© Copyright 2006 Dorsey Brothers Music Limited.
All Rights Reserved. International Copyright Secured.

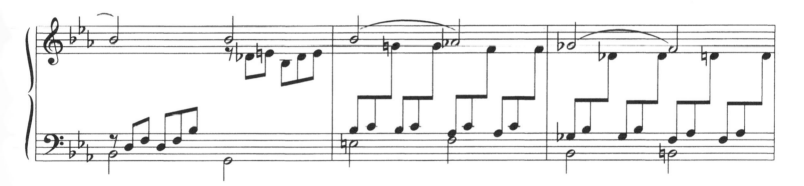

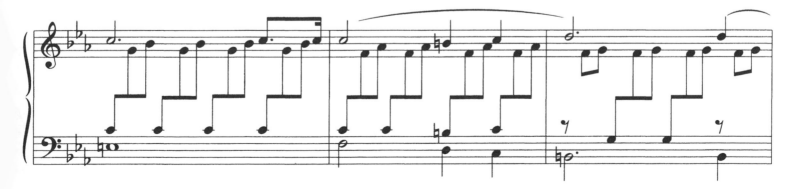

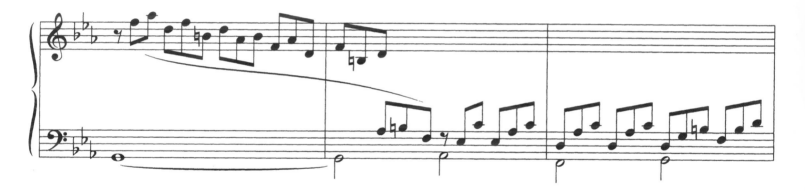

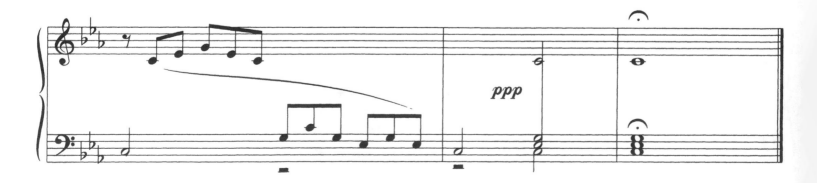

Morning
(from Peer Gynt)

Music by Edvard Grieg

Not too fast

© Copyright 2006 Dorsey Brothers Music Limited.
All Rights Reserved. International Copyright Secured.

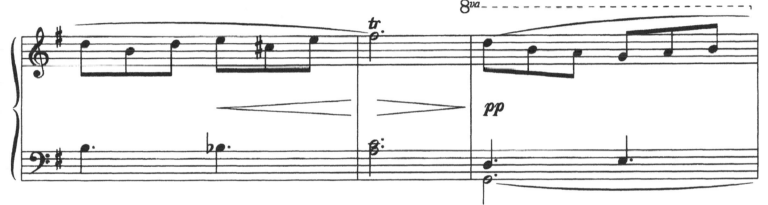

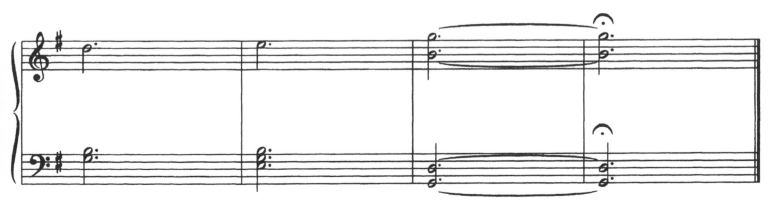

Ode To Joy
(from Symphony No.9 'Choral', Fourth Movement)

Music by Ludwig Van Beethoven

With movement

© Copyright 2006 Dorsey Brothers Music Limited.
All Rights Reserved. International Copyright Secured.

Panis Angelicus

Music by César Franck

Moderately

© Copyright 2006 Dorsey Brothers Music Limited.
All Rights Reserved. International Copyright Secured.

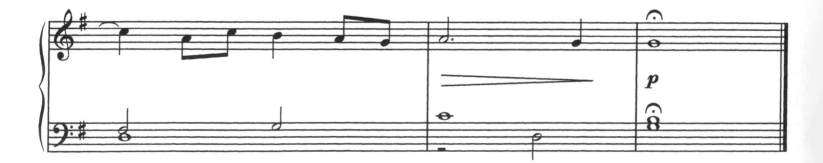

The Pearl Fishers
(Duet: Au Fond Du Temple Saint)

Music by Georges Bizet

Moderately

© Copyright 2006 Dorsey Brothers Music Limited.
All Rights Reserved. International Copyright Secured.

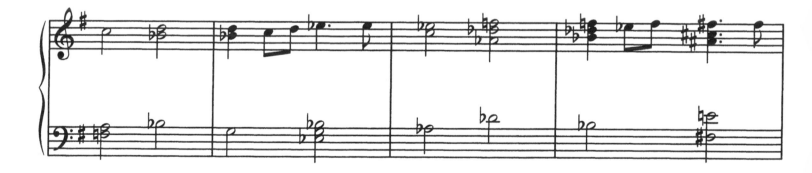

Piano Concerto No.2
(Second Movement Theme)

Music by Frederic Chopin

© Copyright 2006 Dorsey Brothers Music Limited.
All Rights Reserved. International Copyright Secured.

Pie Jesu
(from Requiem, Op.48)

Music by Gabriel Fauré

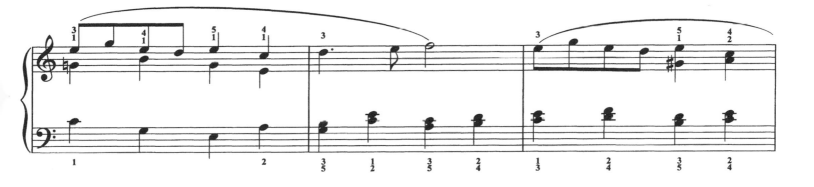

© Copyright 2006 Dorsey Brothers Music Limited.
All Rights Reserved. International Copyright Secured.

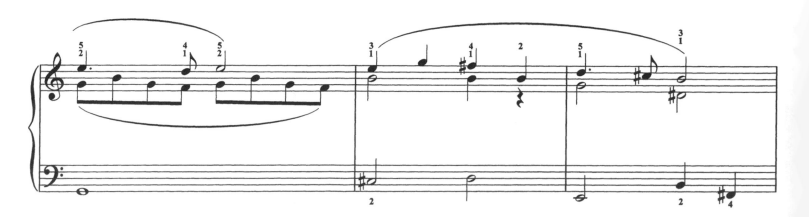

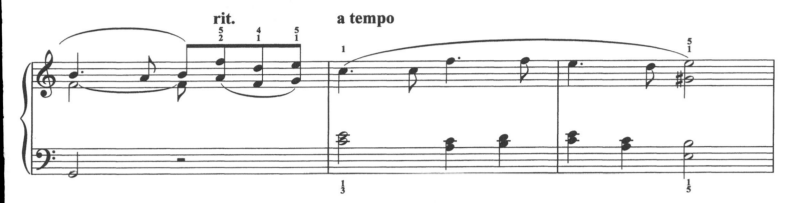

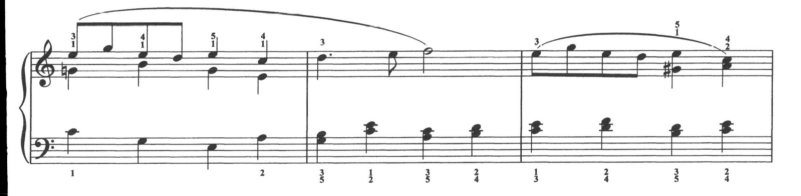

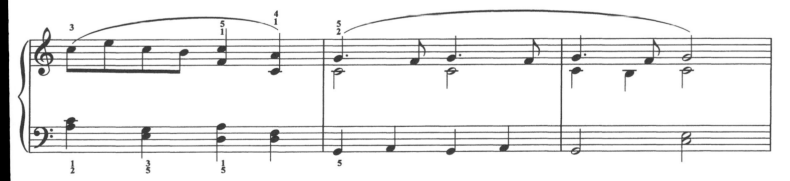

Piano Concerto No.21 'Elvira Madigan'
(Second Movement Theme)

Music by Wolfgang Amadeus Mozart

Slow

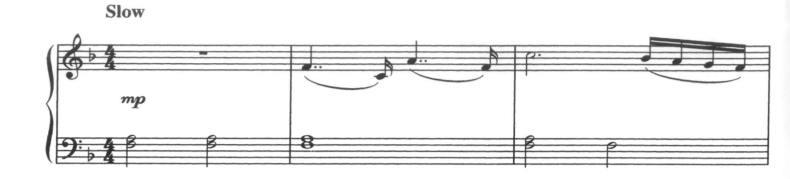

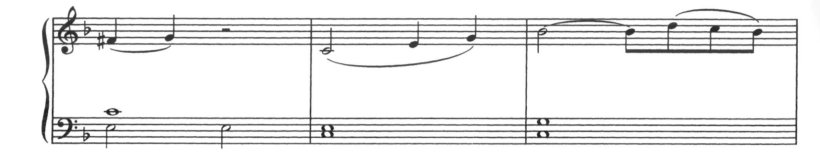

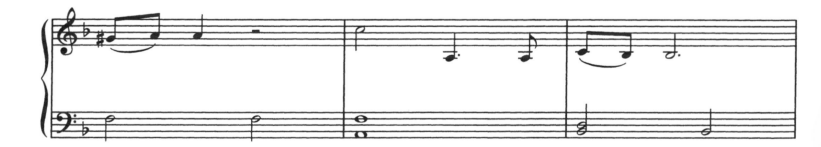

© Copyright 2006 Dorsey Brothers Music Limited.
All Rights Reserved. International Copyright Secured.

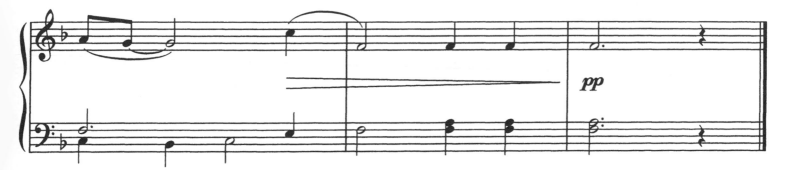

Pictures At An Exhibition

(Promenade)

Music by Modest Mussorgsky

Allegro giusto, nel modo Russico, senza allegreza, ma poco sostenuto

© Copyright 2006 Dorsey Brothers Music Limited.
All Rights Reserved. International Copyright Secured.

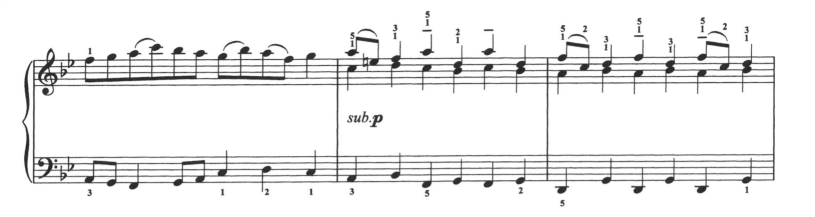

Swan Lake

(Waltz)

Music by Peter Ilyich Tchaikovsky

Moderately

© Copyright 2006 Dorsey Brothers Music Limited.
All Rights Reserved. International Copyright Secured.

Symphony No.5
(First Movement Theme)

Music by Ludwig Van Beethoven

Fairly fast

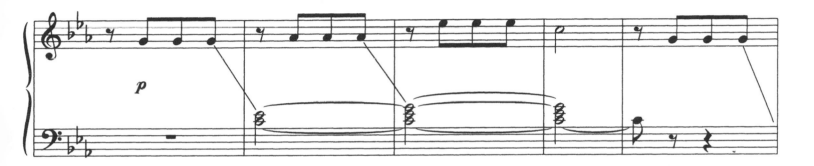

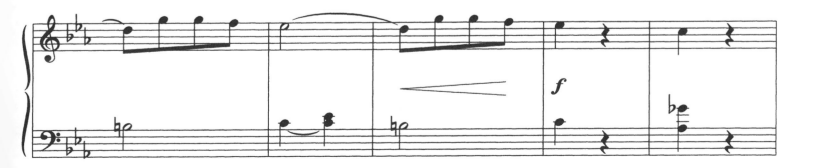

© Copyright 2006 Dorsey Brothers Music Limited.
All Rights Reserved. International Copyright Secured.

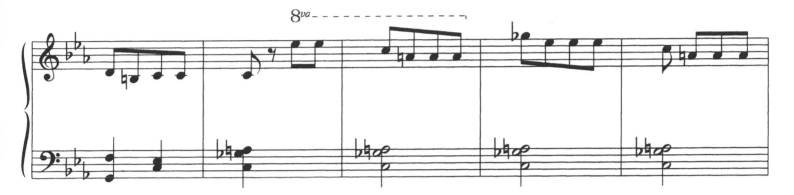

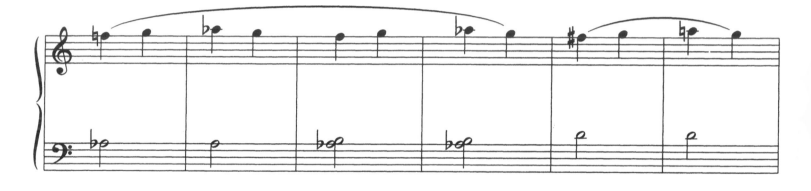

Symphony No.5
(Fourth Movement Theme)

Music by Gustav Mahler

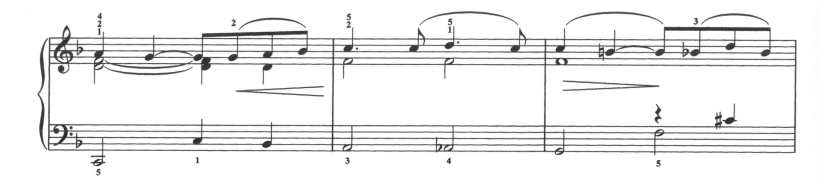

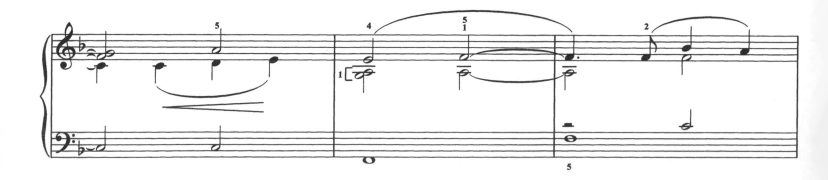

© Copyright 2006 Dorsey Brothers Music Limited.
All Rights Reserved. International Copyright Secured.

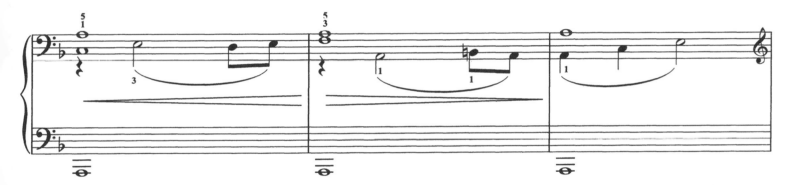

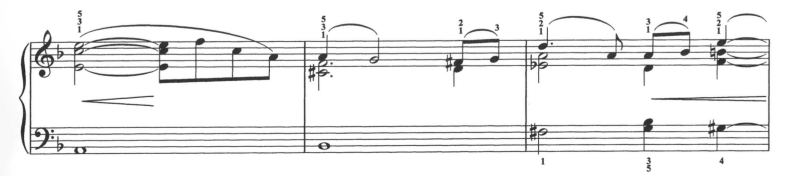

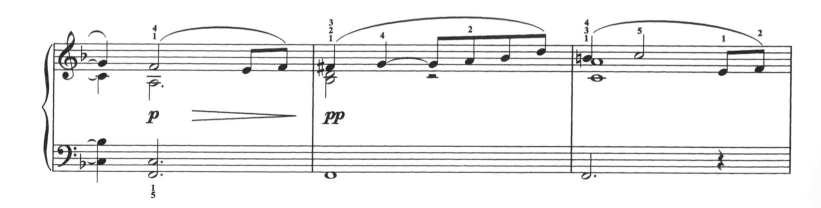

Symphony No.6 'Pastoral'
(Finale Theme)

Music by Ludwig Van Beethoven

Not too fast

© Copyright 2006 Dorsey Brothers Music Limited.
All Rights Reserved. International Copyright Secured.

Symphony No.8 'Unfinished'
(First Movement Theme)

Music by Franz Schubert

Moderato

© Copyright 2006 Dorsey Brothers Music Limited.
All Rights Reserved. International Copyright Secured.

Violin Concerto No.1
(Second Movement Theme)

Music by Max Bruch

Adagio ♩ = 64

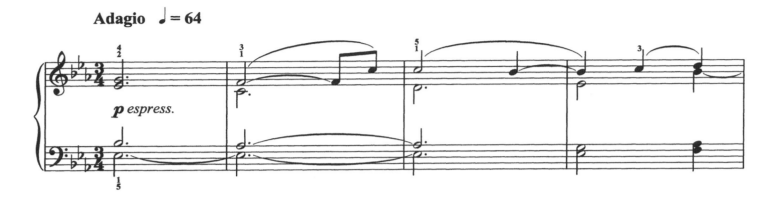

© Copyright 2006 Dorsey Brothers Music Limited.
All Rights Reserved. International Copyright Secured.

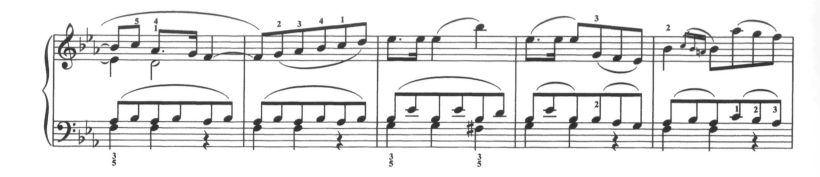

rit.   a tempo

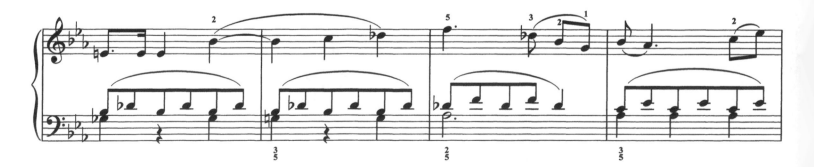

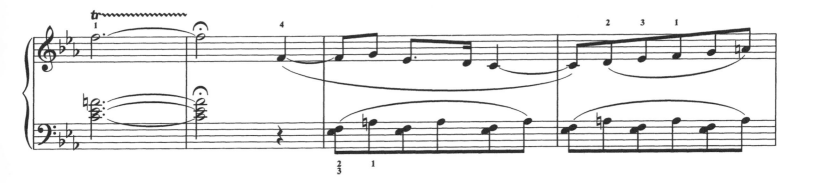

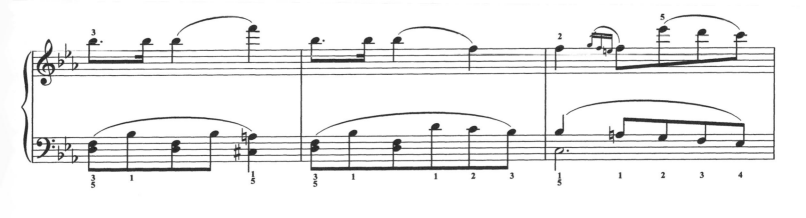

The Water Music

(Air)

Music by George Frideric Handel

Fairly slow

© Copyright 2006 Dorsey Brothers Music Limited.
All Rights Reserved. International Copyright Secured.

William Tell: Overture

Music by Gioacchino Rossini

Bright

© Copyright 2006 Dorsey Brothers Music Limited.
All Rights Reserved. International Copyright Secured.

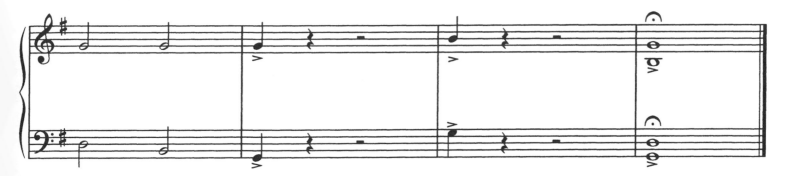

Waltz Of The Flowers
(from The Nutcracker)

Music by Peter Ilyich Tchaikovsky

Valse Moderato

© Copyright 2006 Dorsey Brothers Music Limited.
All Rights Reserved. International Copyright Secured.